Greater Than a Tourist Book Series Reviews from Readers

I think the series is wonderful and beneficial for tourists to get information before visiting the city.

-Seckin Zumbul, Izmir Turkey

I am a world traveler who has read many trip guides but this one really made a difference for me. I would call it a heartfelt creation of a local guide expert instead of just a guide.

-Susy, Isla Holbox, Mexico

New to the area like me, this is a must have!

-Joe, Bloomington, USA

This is a good series that gets down to it when looking for things to do at your destination without having to read a novel for just a few ideas.

-Rachel, Monterey, USA

Good information to have to plan my trip to this destination.

-Pennie Farrell, Mexico

Aptly titled, you won't just be a tourist after reading this book. You'll be greater than a tourist!

-Alan Warner, Grand Rapids, USA

Thank you for a fantastic book.

-Don, Philadelphia, USA

EVANS

Great ideas for a port day.
-Mary Martin USA

Even though I only have three days to spend in San Miguel in an upcoming visit, I will use the author's suggestions to guide some of my time there. An easy read - with chapters named to guide me in directions I want to go.
-Robert Catapano, USA

Great insights from a local perspective! Useful information and a very good value!
-Sarah, USA

This series provides an in-depth experience through the eyes of a local. Reading these series will help you to travel the city in with confidence and it'll make your journey a unique one.
-Andrew Teoh, Ipoh, Malaysia

Tourists can get an amazing "insider scoop" about a lot of places from all over the world. While reading, you can feel how much love the writer put in it.
-Vanja Živković, Sremski Karlovci, Serbia

>TOURIST

GREATER THAN A TOURIST - ATLANTA GEORGIA USA

50 Travel Tips from a Local

Elizabeth Evans

EVANS

Greater Than a Tourist- Atlanta Georgia USA Copyright © 2017 by Lisa Rusczyk. All Rights Reserved.

All rights reserved. No part of this book may be reproduced in any form or by any electronic or mechanical means including information storage and retrieval systems, without permission in writing from the author. The only exception is by a reviewer, who may quote short excerpts in a review.

Cover designed by

Greater Than a Tourist
Visit our website at www.GreaterThanaTourist.com

Lock Haven, PA
All rights reserved.

ISBN: 9781973540991

>TOURIST
50 TRAVEL TIPS FROM A LOCAL

EVANS

BOOK DESCRIPTION

Are you excited about planning your next trip?
Do you want to try something new?
Would you like some guidance from a local?

If you answered yes to any of these questions, then this Greater Than a Tourist book is for you.

Greater Than A Tourist by Elizabeth Evans offers the inside scoop on Atlanta Georgia. Most travel books tell you how to travel like a tourist. Although there is nothing wrong with that, as part of the Greater Than a Tourist series, this book will give you travel tips from someone who has lived at your next travel destination.

In these pages you'll discover advice that will help you throughout your stay. This book will not tell you exact addresses or store hours but instead will give you excitement and knowledge from a local that you may not find in other smaller print travel books.

Travel like a local. Low down, stay in one place, and get to know the people and the culture. By the time you finish this book, you will be eager and prepared to travel to your next destination.

EVANS

>TOURIST

TABLE OF CONTENTS

BOOK DESCRIPTION
TABLE OF CONTENTS
DEDICATION
ABOUT THE AUTHOR
HOW TO USE THIS BOOK
FROM THE PUBLISHER
OUR STORY
WELCOME TO
> TOURIST
INTRODUCTION
1. Edgewood
2. Beltline
3. Octane coffee
4. Cabbagetown
5. Center for Civil and human rights museum
6. Music midtown
7. Shaky knees
8. Piedmont park
9. Kennesaw Mountain
10. Alive after five
11. Canton street roswell
12. Mercedes stadium
13. Shoot the hooch
14. Farmers market
15. Waffle house
16. Chick fil a

EVANS

17. Little five points
18. Freedom Parkway
19. Laughing skull & Vortex
20. Facet Gallery
21. Six flags over georgia
22. Chattahoochee Coffee Company
23. Old Fourth Ward
24. Varsity
25. Georgia tech
26. Delta Museum
27. High museum
28. Center stage
29. Braves baseball
30. The optimist
31. Monday night brewery
32. Sweetwater 420
33. Orpheus
34. Terminal west
35. Tabernacle
36. Iberian Pig
37. Ponce city market
38. Woodstock
39. Ember yoga
40. Marietta Square
41. Decatur Yoga Pilates
42. Atlanta Botanical Gardens
43. Martin Luther King Jr.
44. Fox theatre
45. Stone Summit

46. Sweetwater 420 fest
47. Centennial park
48. Sweet auburn
49. West egg
50. Painted pin

TOP REASONS TO BOOK THIS TRIP

> TOURIST

GREATER THAN A TOURIST

> TOURIST

GREATER THAN A TOURIST

Notes

EVANS

>TOURIST

DEDICATION

This book is dedicated to the dreamers. Dream big, and travel often!

EVANS

ABOUT THE AUTHOR

Elizabeth is a young nomad who loves to travel slow and live large. She enjoys the benefits of traveling near and far, exploring contrasting experiences between city life and open countryside.

Elizabeth spent the first 23 years of her life born and raised in the Atlanta area. Georgia is her home state, and an area she is fond of visiting. After going to high school on the south side of Atlanta, and attending college on the north side, she considers the greater city area to be her hometown.

Elizabeth attended Kennesaw State University where she spent a semester abroad as an exchange student in Amsterdam. There she would her now husband, and ultimate change her life forever. She lives in Finland now with her native spouse, and together they travel Europe often, usually on weekend trips.

Traveling has always been a passion of hers, but writing was an evolved love that came later. After keeping years of journals and an agenda with a daily record of her activities, the art of sharing became more natural. Even more, it became a way to reflect and remember moments. Souvenirs are great, but the moments that happen between transactions, the jokes that sometimes get forgotten, or just writing down the amazing weather that day, have become cherished tokens from her journey.

EVANS

She hopes to share some of those tokens with you in this book. With her personal touch, she describes the city of Atlanta that she grew to know and love deeply.

The best tip to share with you would be to completely immerse yourself in the city. And that doesn't just mean making friends with locals at the bar or in the coffee shop. That means, put the phone down, turn off the music in your ears, and be where you are. Being present whilst traveling doesn't mean you have to be stone cold sober. What it means to her, and many others, is to be present and aware.

Take the time to listen, feel, smell, and embrace the experience you're currently experiencing. Sometimes it can be more invigorating that a beer or any other stimulant. Let the experience of traveling ignite your senses and let you feel the natural high of being in a new environment.

This is her best advice to share with any traveler, from beginner to seasoned veteran. It has helped her throughout her journeys', and ultimately made the difference from basic travel to electric experiences. If you like more of her advice, and want to follow what she is doing now, check out her blog, Nasty Trash on Wordpress at www.nastytrash.blog. So without further a due, here are the top 50 things to do in Atlanta Georgia, as told by Elizabeth Evans.

HOW TO USE THIS BOOK

The Greater Than a Tourist book series was written by someone who has lived in an area for over three months. The goal of this book is to help travelers either dream or experience different locations by providing opinions from a local. The author has made suggestions based on their own experiences. Please do your own research before traveling to the area in case the suggested places are unavailable.

EVANS

FROM THE PUBLISHER

Traveling can be one of the most important parts of a person's life. The anticipation and memories that you have are some of the best. As a publisher of the Greater Than a Tourist book series, as well as the popular 50 Things to Know book series, we strive to help you learn about new places, spark your imagination, and inspire you. Wherever you are and whatever you do I wish you safe, fun, and inspiring travel.

Lisa Rusczyk Ed. D.
CZYK Publishing

EVANS

OUR STORY

Traveling is a passion of the "Greater than a Tourist" series creator. Lisa studied abroad in college, and for their honeymoon Lisa and her husband toured Europe. During her travels to Malta, an older man tried to give her some advice based on his own experience living on the island since he was a young boy. She was not sure if she should talk to the stranger but was interested in his advice. When traveling to some places she was wary to talk to locals because she was afraid that they weren't being genuine. Through her travels, Lisa learned how much locals had to share with tourists. Lisa created the "Greater Than a Tourist" book series to help connect people with locals. A topic that locals are very passionate about sharing.

EVANS

WELCOME TO
> TOURIST

EVANS

>TOURIST

INTRODUCTION

Few seconds in life are more releasing than those in which a plane ascends into the sky. Looking out a window from inside a machine standing stationary at the beginning of a runway, we face a vista of familiar proportions. Then suddenly, accompanied by the controlled rage of the engines, we rise fluently into the atmosphere, and an immense horizon opens up across which we can wander without impediment.
Alain de Botton, from The Art of Travel

Welcome to Atlanta! Life in the furthest suburb of New York City is pretty sweet. Southern traditions meet urban living and add up to a comfortable place to explore, eat, and make memories! This guide is designed to give you the best of it all. Whether you have a strict budget or the means to experience everything, I have thought of something for you to do in Atlanta.

My favorite way to get into the city is by plane. Although driving is possible, flying just gives the best preview for the adventure ahead. As you descend into Hartsfield Jackson Airport you can already begin to visualize the city in Technicolor. No matter your means of transportation, it is nevertheless a welcoming place to be.

EVANS

The following list of things to do is in no order or favoritism, but simply the things I enjoyed the most when living in the Atlanta area. A nickname for Atlanta is the city of trees, so with that in mind, I invite you to wander of the beaten path, and make an adventure of your own! There is plenty of urban and rural to explore all within I-285, and a little more just outside!

I will warn you, after your trip you may experience a few withdraws, primarily of the impeccable food scene. You may also notice your taste in music grow, considering that some of the best and original music comes from these streets. Or at least you can listen to it on the radio while sitting in traffic on I-85 trying to get to Midtown. Either way, Atlanta has a lasting impression, and you will not regret the time spent in this city. I know John Mayer, Ray Charles, and Usher sure benefit from their time here, not to mention the countless others who love this city and all of its glory.

So without slowing you down any longer, lets get started with the list of things to do in Atlanta Georgia!

1. EDGEWOOD

Starting off simple, let me welcome you to the neighborhood of Edgewood Atlanta. East Atlanta has architecturally remained the same for decades. This area has great photogenic potential as well as plenty to do while you wander its streets. The night life is fun and vivacious, while the day time is reserved and simple. Life here is balanced keeping all walks of life entertained.

More specifically, Edgewood Avenue is my favorite place to hangout. For evening drinks or just to get out and get involved with the city, this is a great place to be. I like MOTHER for a drink on the patio. Or just up the road, you can go to Sister Louisa's Church of the Living Room & Ping Pong Emporium. This place isn't for the faint of heart, and it is not for reasons you may be thinking. The decor and style of this place are for those with a good sense of humor, and like the darker parts of life. Personally, I think this place is freaking amazing!

2. BELTLINE

In recent years, the city has renovated old train track lines into urban pathways. These trails cover 22 miles and are a great way to explore the city. Walk, bike, or stop to enjoy the scenic views, the beltline is sure to entertain you on a beautiful day in the A!

If you are interested in the perfect picture, there are a few spots along the path to get that good-looking sunset picture. Golden hour will not go wasted wandering this part of the city.

Also, be sure to look into local art exhibits being featured on the trail. Native artists frequently show their work and constantly change the atmosphere of the Beltline. Works such as sculpture, murals, and instillations are constantly on display here. Learn more about Atlanta's local artists and their work whilst enjoying the beautiful Beltline.

>TOURIST

3. OCTANE COFFEE

When you are in need of a caffeine fix, or need something a little stronger, Octane Coffee has what you need. This trendy little café will serve some of the finest drinks you can get in East Atlanta. Growing rapidly, this local favorite now has six locations in the city. My favorite location is the Grant Park spot. Be sure to plan enough time for this coffee break though, seating is limited and tends to stay busy during open hours.

It is also rumored that some of the local celebrities like to get their caffeine fix here. So, if you're a fan of Atlanta movie and television productions, it may be worth your while to steak out the area. Be kind to those who create your favorite content, but don't feel ashamed to praise their work if you happen to cross paths.

4. CABBAGETOWN

Another must see neighborhood is Cabbagetown. Filled with murals, small shops, and old architecture, a walking tour will keep you entertained for the afternoon. Rain or shine, this neighborhood is a cozy little corner of the city worth exploring.

Make your way over to Wylie Street for some awesome urban art. The wall boarding the road is covered in murals and constantly changing. Local artists embrace the city canvas and make it their own.

Or grad a bite to eat at Agave located at the corner of Carroll Street and the Boulevard. This southwestern style restaurant is sure to appease the appetite after hours of wandering ATL.

5. CENTER FOR CIVIL AND HUMAN RIGHTS MUSEUM

Taking things a bit more traditional, Atlanta has a great selection of museums. It is also the heart of some of the countries most powerful civil rights movements. Visit this wonderfully organized facility and spend some time learning about where the city has come from and where it plans to go! Also, check their website for the latest special news updates regarding seasonal exhibits.

I visited this place for the first time with my sister in 2015. It was an overwhelming experience. Some of the exhibits then have since changed, but the root message here is the same. The goal here is, "to connect the American Civil Rights Movement to today's Global Human Rights Movements". As shocking as some of the exhibits may be, it is an overall inspiring experience and an Atlanta must see museum.

6. MUSIC MIDTOWN

For anyone who likes to party this festival is sure to impress. At the end of every summer, the city hosts one of the largest urban music festivals right in the middle of the city for three days. Located in the popular and scenic area of Piedmont Park, Music Midtown is the place to be seen. With lineups varying in artists from Red Hot Chili Peppers, Bruno Marz, Arctic Monkeys, and even Billy Idol. With such an eclectic variety of music, everyone is sure to enjoy this iconic event.

Some of my favorite concert performances have happened at Music Midtown. I will never forget the time I saw Imagine Dragons perform special rendition of Stand By Me. Or just hours before, when Weezer took a break during their set to give a shout out to Peachtree City, my hometown!

If you do plan to attend this festival, be aware that is easily accessible by the Beltline. So if you can plan to get there by walking or biking, I would high suggest avoiding public transportation or driving traffic. You will thank me later when you can easily hop on your bike and get out of there when the show is over.

7. SHAKY KNEES

Another music festival? Yes! A newer festival, but quickly growing in size, this event is just as impressive. Shaky knee festival hosts more nontraditional music and entertains fans for a full weekend. If you need a break from the rockin' bands, there are loads of food vendors to keep you satisfied in between sets. Be sure to check out this years line up for your chance to get in on the fun.

8. PIEDMONT PARK

What is better than a beautiful day in the city? Well, walk over to Piedmont Park to really soak up all the fun in the sun. This green area stretches across midtown and hosts sport games, dog walkers, sunbathers, and the infamous Instagramers.

A little history about this park, it opened in 1895! It is open all year round and through out the 189 acres you can find amazing views of the city. The Lake Clara Meer dock was added later, but is a beautiful area to enjoy the city skyline amongst nature. This city truly provides the best of both worlds, adding nature and urban in the same moments. Here at the dock you can really feel the balance of these two worlds come together.

9. KENNESAW MOUNTAIN

If you need a break from the hustle of the city, just take a 20minute drive to Kennesaw Mountain for a peaceful hike. Once at the top, you will get a spectacular view of Atlanta to the south, and to the north, the North Georgia hills are closer than you would imagine.

Also a historic part of the city, Kennesaw Mountain was the site of some of the countries most controversial scenes. With a museum at the entrance of the park, you can quickly learn more about the entire history of the land. As well as, throughout your hike, enjoy the scenic canons and memorabilia left on the mountain. Despite your interests in history, or physical activity, this hike is worth it. My tip, plan to spend the morning during a weekday. You are sure to miss most of the traffic this way, and you will be done by noon to carry on exploring the greater city area.

I spent many afternoons and early mornings hiking here during my undergrad days. Rain or shine, it is great place to get out, get moving, and enjoy nature. And as I mentioned before, the reward is the most stunning panoramic view of the Atlanta skyline. You will want to be sure to have your camera phone ready or snap a photo to share online.

>TOURIST

10. ALIVE AFTER FIVE

In the neighborhood of Roswell, Alive After Five is a seasonal event that hosts a plethora of food, drinks, and fun. Get in on the action between April and October on the third Thursday of every month. If your travel dates do not coordinate, don't be dismayed, the area hosts loads of fun the rest of the time!

The concurrent festival welcomes guests to a lively evening of music, food trucks and fun for all. Explore historic Roswell whist enjoying the best of southern city living.

11. CANTON STREET ROSWELL

Like I said, there is loads of fun to be had all the time! The small shops, unique restaurants, and picturesque road will slip you right into a southern dream. The people in the community love to host. If you need help ordering a drink, or taking a selfie, the people on Main Street are the reason why it is so special!

One of my favorite places is the Ceviche Taqueria & Margarita Bar. You can trust this place has some of the best margaritas in town. I mean, they have it in the name! Stop by for happy hour, or stay for a meal. Your taste buds will thank you.

Another great place is Table & Main. I could go on and on about how great this place is, and all the memories made here. From the outside, it appears to be just a small traditional style home. This renovated piece of history serves up a lot more than southern nostalgia. The food is outstanding, and the bar staff is sure to keep you entertained.

Just across the street, the owner has another gem, Osteria Mattone. A more formal experience, you are in for a treat at this traditional Italian restaurant. It is the perfect place to celebrate a birthday, anniversary, or any other special occasion. I would suggest staying for a full meal, all the way till dessert. Absolutely everything is of amazing quality and just an overall wonderful dinning experience.

>TOURIST

12. MERCEDES STADIUM

This is the cities newest attraction. Depending on whether you are traveling during football or soccer season be sure to watch a game at the new and improved sports stadium. You will not regret attending and getting a chance to explore this modern marvel.

Before 2017, the Atlanta Falcons football team played at the Georgia Dome. Here, fans would gather for events between 1992 and till its final event in 2017. Demolition took place on November 20, 2017, and the site will be renovated to be a green space for tailgating.

The Mercedes Stadium is rumored to be the cities bid to host future Super Bowl games. It was supposedly said that the city of Atlanta would not host another Super Bowl until renovating or rebuilding another stadium.

No matter if you are traveling through Atlanta for a Super Bowl game, or just want to see an event here, this new arena is impressive. Rise up with the Atlanta Falcons, or check out our latest team, the Atlanta United FC, and cheer on with locals alike.

13. SHOOT THE HOOCH

For the summer travelers, this is for you! Get your friends, a six pack, and something inflatable, and head over to the Chattahoochee River that runs right through the city. Here, you can tie your rafts together, with your drinks, and spend a day floating down the river with your best friends making a one of a kind memory!

There are three different routes to take when you Shoot The Hooch. The first route is only 1.5 miles. This would take the lesser part of an afternoon and be lots of fun. The second route is 3 miles long. Finally, the longest route is 8 miles. For the true adventure crew, this is your thing!

Choose to bring a raft, canoe, kayak, or SUP. It is really whatever floats your boat! Ha! You can make reservations easily by visiting their website or making a call. Email is also available.

>TOURIST

14. FARMERS MARKET

A great way to get to know the community is by exploring local Farmers Markets. My personal favorite is the Grant Park Farmers Market. A mix of food, local goods, and music, it is a family friendly experience for all to enjoy.

Your Dekalb Farmers Market is open every day from 9:00am to 9:00pm and is a wild and wonderful place to explore. With foods and spices from all around the world, it is way more than just a local market. Here you can get a shopping experience like no other. No matter where you are from, you will feel welcome here with national flags hanging from the ceiling to decorate the space.

Farmers Markets are a great way to explore the city if you are traveling on a budget. Samples are a usual pleasure, and other amenities such as musical entertainment tend to make the day better. Don't worry if you aren't in need of groceries, most markets these days sell local made crafts and goods too.

15. WAFFLE HOUSE

You cannot go to Atlanta and not eat at Waffle House. Walk in, say hey to everyone, and order yourself an All-Star with a sweet tea. Don't worry about making a reservation, they are open 24/7, and there is always something interesting happening.

There is nothing more "Atlanta" than having a classic Waffle House story. No matter if you go for breakfast after church, need cheap and massive meal, or want to eat the whole kitchen at 4am, this is your heaven! I swear, every time I leave Atlanta, this is the one place I miss the most. The stories, the food, and the people make it an experience in itself.

16. CHICK FIL A

Speaking of iconic local food, did you know the Chick Fil A Chicken Sandwich was invented in Atlanta Georgia. Check out the original location, or go to any other hundreds of locations across the greater city area. Just don't go on Sunday, unlike Waffle House, Chick Fil A does take a day off to rest.

The Original Chick Fil A Dwarf house is a fan favorite. The peculiar building welcomes families to an authentic dine in experience. Whilst still getting all of your favorite fried chicken meals, children, and young spirited adults can enjoy all the Dwarf House experience has to offer.

Food aside, the Chick Fil A mission is to please customers with an exceptional experience. I have never met a soul who hasn't enjoyed the service from eating here. The company has truly set the standard for best serving its guests and improving the lives of their employees.

17. LITTLE FIVE POINTS

Another neighborhood worth exploring is Little Five Points. This area is eclectic, edgy, and where the odd ball calls home. I love this neighborhood because it is full of character, stories, and interesting things. Spend an afternoon or the better part of the day here. Just be sure to secure a parking spot, spaces are limited!

This area is one of my favorite places to visit. I can remember in High School, skipping class and driving to Little Five Points with my friends to hang out for the afternoon. We were too young to go to any bars, or even get tattoos, but the area was edgy enough to make us feel like we were already adults.

The favorite store I always love to visit time and time again is 42 Degrees. It is a special little glass shop with local art as well as pieces from around the country. The unique deign and special quality detailing makes it a one of a kind shopping experience.

Another one of a kind experience, and unique in its own right, is just across the street. Junkman's Daughter is a larger store, hosting a variety of quirky non-traditional memorabilia and kitschy gifts. Like Spencer's Gift Shop on steroids, Junkman's Daughter is always open to entertain. No matter if you need a Halloween costume, gag gift, or just something special and a bit odd, this place has it!

Lastly,

18. FREEDOM PARKWAY

Somewhere between Cabbagetown and Little Five Points, is Freedom Parkway. If you Google "Atlanta" odds are you have seen pictures of the city from this very street. So if you too are looking for that famous picture, or just take a drive down this way and you will see it for yourself. Plus, if any of you are Walking Dead fans, you will not want to miss this photo opportunity! Remember the season 1 poster; well the view right here inspired that scene. It would later be recreated, not to be ironic, during the 2014 snowstorm.

19. LAUGHING SKULL & VORTEX

With two locations in the city, this comedy club will be a must during your visit. No matter if you are there for a show, or just need a beer, this place is easy to find. With a unique sense of décor and branding, the space itself is enough to keep someone entertained.

A perfect night would include a couple pints whilst enjoying a comedy show. Then after spending the evening dining and drinking the night away. This place is casual enough to make anyone feel right at home. Enjoy the alternative environment to traditional entertainment and get your laugh on!

20. FACET GALLERY

If you enjoy local artists, or don't fit in with the preppy Buckhead scene, head over to Facet Gallery for one of their art shows. With the constantly changing exhibits, there is sure to be something new every time you come to Atlanta. Founded by a few Atlanta locals, this place is a diamond in the rough. Follow Face Gallery on Instagram to learn more about their latest exhibits or events.

21. SIX FLAGS OVER GEORGIA

Need an adrenaline rush after sitting in traffic all morning? Look no further than the cities own Six Flags. Feel like a kid again wandering the Looney Tune themed park and getting a head rush from all the rides. Fun for all ages, and the park is easily found in the city.

This facility is truly local landmark. After opening the gates in 1967, the park has been a source of fun for the whole family for decades. Located just west of the Chattahoochee River, this amusement park is truly a famous part of the city.

>TOURIST

22. CHATTAHOOCHEE COFFEE COMPANY

This is my best-kept secret from all my years of living in Atlanta. This place takes a little work to find, but for the true adventurer, it will not disappoint. Right smack dab in the middle of the city, there is a perfect coffee shop nestled beautifully by the river. Literally a 2-minute drive from one of the biggest highways, you will think you are somewhere 3 hours north of the city. Take a break from the concrete jungle, or simple come for the best coffee of your life, it is a rejuvenating experience.

Some of my favorite memories of the city begin right here in this coffee shop. It is a magical location. Spending hours working away on my computer next to the river is so relaxing. It is also a tranquil environment to catch up with family or friends. Although the directions can be a bit testing, the reward is a beautiful backdrop for conversing.

23. OLD FOURTH WARD

This particular road is for the photographers, history buffs, and trendy travelers. I love this place for being one of the most beautiful drives on the south side of the city. Drive by, or stop along the way to get lunch at a local eatery, this place is a lovely adventure and easy to find!

Some hot spots in this area include the Historic Fourth Ward Park. Spend some time here by the pond or just take a scenic route on your commute to enjoy the neighborhood.

Another favorite location is the Historic Fourth Ward Skate Park. It is simply a cozy place to hang out in the area and also enjoy the local activity. Adults and kids alike are welcome to enjoy to local activities partaking here outside.

24. VARSITY

There isn't much else that is more iconic than The Varsity. Serving customers since 1929, it is history in a burger. Although, my personal favorite is their chocolate milk shakes! The building has been on the same corner for decades. Serving up the same classic, and passing out those famous red and white hats for guests to wear and enjoy.

25. GEORGIA TECH

Simple walk over the bridge on your way out from The Varsity and you are on the Georgia Tech campus! This beautiful university hosts an abundance of brick buildings and beautiful sights. Take a wander around, or plan a visit to one of their football games for a true local experience.

I would highly suggest attending one of the nationally ranked basketball games right here in the city. Tech fans sure know how to get their buzz on! Or if it is football season, enjoy the great outdoors in downtown Atlanta! That's right, their football stadium is in the center of the city! As sports and fun progress around you, enjoy the Atlanta skyline above and around you. It is a special experience, especially when you get a W for the home team.

26. DELTA MUSEUM

If you have ever been to the Hartsfield Jackson Atlanta Airport, odds are you may have noticed Delta Airlines in a few places. Well that is because the airline company was founded right there where you are walking. You can tour their history museum, located just across the runway. Learn how a little farming family turned a crop plane into a mega corporation and international airline. Just cruise on over to the Delta Headquarter Offices on the other side of the airport and learn all about this visionary company!

Be sure to sign up in advance to take a flight simulation, the same one the pilots take! Or take a tour of the retired planes. Walk through air travel history as Delta teaches you everything about world class travel.

27. HIGH MUSEUM

Another museum worth checking out is the HIGH. A modern building with impressive collections and priceless works of art, this experience is sure to impress any art enthusiast. Be sure to check out student prices and special exhibits before planning your visit.

The High has so many eclectic events and special exhibits. I remember one year in particular when my step sister, a jewelry designer and creator of Ashley Buchanan Jewelry, had the change to show her work for one special evening.

Other activities and more hands on events are happening all the time too. If this sort of thing interests you, follow The High on Instagram or online to keep up with the activities.

28. CENTER STAGE

This venue has something going on every day of the week. From comedy shows, music performances, local artists, and even church services. Center Stage is conveniently located in the middle of the city and easy to access. There is no reason to miss a show when venues like this are busy 7 days a week all year long.

29. BRAVES BASEBALL

After opening the brand new SunTrust Park in 2017, this place is way more than a sports venue. Luck for you, baseball season lasts nearly 9 months of the year, so odds are there is a game during your trip. Wander the shops, restaurants, and enjoy one of Americas greatest past times.

The retired field has been taken over by the local Georgia State University. Home to the braves from 1997-2016, the once thriving field now belongs to the university. Still, the baseball park hosts a load of history for you die hard fans. The parking lot, for instance, is designed around original field, and the concrete wall surrounding the area is the first outfield perimeter.

No matter if you are a fan of the sport or not, a baseball game is much more than that. The experience includes families and friends to take a break from their lives and come together for a few hours. Become part of the community instantly simply by attending the game. Account for a few extra hours tailgating before and you will feel like a local before the first pitch!

30. THE OPTIMIST

While visiting the city, be sure to check out the best oyster bar in town. The owners have a few locations, but this places takes the cake. Famous oysters put you in a trance, and if you need to take a break from all the greatness, just step outside for a quick round of mini golf! Yes that's right, this place also has mini golf!

31. MONDAY NIGHT BREWERY

Nestled on a lot of trees, smack dab in the middle of the city, Monday Night Brewery is the place for fun lovers. Enjoy local beer with friends, and explore this warehouse-converted fun house! Play corn hole, take a selfie with the infamous tie wall, or just sip on a great IPA, your not going to leave without a smile on your face after spending an evening here.

This hot spot stole the hearts of locals with their three iconic brews. Blind Pirate Orange IPA, FU Manbrew, and Drafty Kilt are the first three beers to steal the scene. Since opening their doors nearly 5 years ago, the selection has grown and you can even enjoy the occasional seasonal brew depending on what time of year it is.

>TOURIST

32. SWEETWATER 420

As the poster child for Atlanta beer, Sweetwater 420 Brewery is a must. You can take a tour of the facility while sipping on your own brew. Bring your friends, or come alone and make some new friends. Locals and tourists alike will have a great night hanging out here.

Sweetwater has been around for as long as I can remember. Not only does this beer have a sweet sport in the local community, it is a leading brand that is welcomed at every single Atlanta event. Sports events, music concerts, and most restaurants serve this legendary beer. It is quickly becoming a symbol of Atlanta with the Coca-Cola brand.

33. ORPHEUS

Last but not least in Atlanta brewery's is Orpheus. This one is for the true beer enthusiasts. Check out their tours or plan to make a day of it here. Similar to other brewery's in the area, Orpheus has six year-round beers. Other options rotate based on popularity and season. There is also the occasion to limited. I will say, this place is for the brew lovers. Sample a little of everything, or have a long love with one favorite, the selection is worth the exploration.

34. TERMINAL WEST

As a converted train station, Terminal West is one of my favorite music venues. Wonderful place to catch a music show and wander the grounds and different spaces. Go beyond the dance floor upstairs to the balcony view. Enjoy the show from new heights here. Or take a break from the sweaty scene of the show, and go to the backyard. Here you can grab a little fresh air, and soak in the southern night. A well-decorated garden awaits your discovery as you explore Terminal West.

Bonus, they have a restaurant too! Get to the show early and have dinner here. Be sure to order the fried avocado, it is amazing! As is everything on the menu!

35. TABERNACLE

Probably the most famous music venue in the city, Tabernacle has been around for ages. A true Atlanta native has about a dozen stories regarding this place. Plan your trip early and get tickets to a show before they sell out! You wont regret the experience.

The Tabernacle opened in 1911 and closed for a small period of time between 1991-1996. There was a temporary renovation after an evacuation during a Panic! At the Disco concert. Ironically, the floor had cracked and the show was canceled. No one was injured, but it did make for an interesting headline.

One thing I truly love about this venue, besides the amazing history, is the freedom to explore. Unlike other music halls that simply have a stage and an audience floor, the Tabernacle is different. Nearly four stories tall, there is lots of room to explore. Getting to the venue early is fun when you have dozens of rooms to explore. Take a break from the dancing on the lavish furnishings throughout the building is to me, one of the most exciting parts of a night out at the Tabernacle. Small bar areas are tucked away, so if the line is too long, or you simply want to talk with your friends. Don't worry about missing the show, every space is equipped with a live feed TV of the show.

36. IBERIAN PIG

Another restaurant worth a meal is the Iberian Pig in Decatur. It has quickly become a local favorite and famous spot in town. Plan a full dinner, or stop by for a quick lunch, the food is impressive all day long. The Spanish themed cuisines is perfectly prepared to be a lovely experience to share with friends, or enjoy all by yourself!

37. PONCE CITY MARKET

As a new addition to an old building, this renovation stole the hearts of Atlanta dwellers. Wander the little shops as you make your way to the rooftop. There you will find games and views to enjoy well into the evening.

To quote the National Trust for Historic Preservation, "Ponce City Market is history in the making". The iconic building is easily found in the center of one of the most eclectic neighborhoods. Not only does this renovated landmark offer activities by day, you can even live here! That's right, if you aren't already in love with Atlanta, you can now live in the center of the scene.

There is so much to enjoy about this resurrection. The energy that lives in this area have a lasting impression on all those who experience this neighborhood. From the easy access to the Beltline, all the way to the rooftops views of that special Atlanta skyline, Ponce City Market is more than just a shopping experience… it is a lifestyle!

38. WOODSTOCK

If you are coming to the south for a proper country experience, make your way north about 25 minutes to the little town of Woodstock. There you can enjoy incredible southern fine dining, great unique shops, and amazing coffees. This picture perfect, one light town is sure to please!

The area is welcoming to anyone, with a fun farmers market on weekends, coffee shops to fuel your mornings, and a lively night scene to pleasure you into the night. It has all the Georgian charm of a southern life, whilst only being a moments drive from the downtown area of Atlanta.

I would specifically suggest the Copper Coin Coffee for anyone looking to catch up with friends, enjoy a good cup of coffee, or needing a quiet place to do a little work. Across the street is the Pure Taqueria Mexican Restaurant. A fun place with great food, enjoy the rooftop area with a great meal, or hang out downstairs at the bar to really have a good time!

39. EMBER YOGA

If tranquility is what you need, spend an extra hour or so in the Woodstock neighborhood to take a yoga class with Ember. Their hot yoga is famous across Atlanta. They have showers too, so after class you can get right back to exploring!

If you do not have time to take a class, no worries! Ember Yoga has a wonderful boutique to browse books, jewelry, apparel, and other goods. Buy a memento for your journey and bring a little peace and tranquility along with you on your travels.

40. MARIETTA SQUARE

More centrally located, you can find the Historic District of Mariette. Check out the Main Square and local goods. You will feel as though you have walked right onto the set of a classic southern movie.

If you enjoy antiquing, there a couple spots to check out and wander for an hour or more. The square also has a couple art galleries if you prefer that sort of interests. To be completely honest, my favorite thing is Niks Place. Far from a gallery, but a relic nonetheless, this is my favorite place to be in Marietta. Just a stones throw from the square, Niks hosts a variety of live music nights, has the friendliest customers, and serves the best gyros I have ever eaten in my life!

>TOURIST

41. DECATUR YOGA PILATES

If you need to get physical, look no further than Decatur. This facility hosts a various amount of classes. The up and coming neighborhood may be over looked by tourists, but remember, you're living like a local!

The Decatur neighborhood has changed over the years, but the heart is still thriving. The love in this neighborhood can be felt as your drive down the tree lined roads. When you are done with the yoga class, be sure to grab a bite to eat. Across the street you can find Farm Burger Decatur. Hands down the best veggie burger in the neighborhood.

42. ATLANTA BOTANICAL GARDENS

Spend some time in the city's botanical gardens. Art installations change throughout the seasons and years. If you happen to be in town around Christmas, you are in for a real treat!

Be sure to check online for the opening hours and special attractions. The Botanical Gardens also do a magical job at creating a beautiful Christmas light display during the holiday season. Seasonal hours do apply, so plan ahead before attending.

My favorite feature by far is the Art In The Garden. This way you are able to enjoy mother nature and man made beauty all at once. One of the most iconic pieces is the Earth Goddess. Originally a temporary installation, the beloved addition became a permanent installation. Earth Goddess now greets guests as they enter the Cascades Garden. At 25 feet high, she is a stunning example of nature and human made creation. As I said before, the gardens become a wonderful Christmas experience, and the Earth Goddess herself gets a make over when she transforms into the Ice Goddess every holiday.

>TOURIST

43. MARTIN LUTHER KING JR.

Atlanta is home to many people, but one man we are most proud of is Mr. Martin Luther King Jr. He was born right here in the city center. You can still visit his childhood home! You can also visit his church, Ebenezer Baptist Church.

If you do not know who Mr. King is, let me give you a little background. During the Civil Rights Movement, MLK gained popularity for his active participation in promoting justice for colored citizens in the United States. Originally a preacher, his way with words captivated more than just Sunday audiences.

He is a true hero to me, and my fellow neighbors and friends in Atlanta. I am proud to have studied his work, mission, and efforts made to bring equality to all.

44. FOX THEATRE

The Fox is one of my favorite buildings in the entire city. Opening in 1929, elegance is in every corner of this lavish theater.

After being named a National Historic Landmark in 1976 due to its distinguishing architectural features, it is easy to see at first glance why this place holds so much value to locals and travelers alike.

Don't worry if you're not a fan of the classical performances, I have a tip for you too. Check out the Saturday morning show where they play classic cartoons. Bring the family, or just come alone if you wish to feel like a kid again. You will be awe struck watching the classics in the famous theatre.

45. STONE SUMMIT

Ranked as one of the best climbing gyms in the United State by Climbing Magazine, Stone Summit is a fun and active experience. With two locations in Atlanta and one in Kennesaw it is easy to make your way over here for some wholesome exercise.

As a hobby climber myself, this is your climbing facility on steroids. My favorite location being the Kennesaw development, opened in 2014, has so much to offer guests. Rent all the equipment you need, or bring your own, and spend the day here till your arms fall off. Don't worry if you need a break, staff is usually pretty friendly about taking an hour off to cruise over to Chipotle for some much needed fuel and returning later to continue the burn!

All locations require you to sign a simple waiver, asking you to kindly behave like an adult and don't do anything stupid or harmful. Then you are ready to climb the day away. Take it easy in the bouldering sections or get some serious air and literally reach for the sky.

46. SWEETWATER 420 FEST

As previously mentioned, Sweetwater is a famous beverage in the south. What is more exciting is the musical festival the company hosts every year in the city. No surprise, the festival tends to fall in April around the 20th. A fun combination of reggae, funk, local rap, and great beer make this festival a must!

I absolutely love this festival. It is different than others that are traditionally hosted by Ticketmaster or large corporations. This one is hosted by the brewery themselves, and it is so much fun. Three days of good vibes, good beers, and the best music. No matter if it is rain or shine, you will have an awesome time here in Centennial Park wandering the three stages, various food trucks, and enjoying the city landscape around you.

In 2014 I attended the three day festival and had a blast! My favorite part was when the Dirty Heads performed on Sunday. It had rained both days prior, and this was the first time the sun had come out and everyone was having a great time. Despite the mud below, the beer within kept the mood light. Afterwards I kept the good times rolling and took a ride on the SkyView Atlanta just across the street from the venue. Looking down on the festival and getting a sunset ride on the Ferris wheel made for a memory I will never forget.

>TOURIST

47. CENTENNIAL PARK

Centennial Park hosts a various amount of activities through the seasons, but no matter what time of year you visit, you must explore this lush green park in the city. Surrounding the park is some of the city's most famous attractions. My favorite thing to do is watch the 4th of July fireworks from the lawn, or maybe ice skating at Christmas time! I can't decide.

Here you are surrounded by some of Atlanta's most famous attractions. As I mentioned before, SkyView Atlanta, the cities Ferris Wheel is just across the street. Within 100 meters of that you are at the entrance of the Coca Cola Museum. If you did not already know, Atlanta is home to the infamous Coca Cola Company and the place where the iconic drink was invented so many years ago.

Just across the yard from the museum is the Georgia Aquarium. This is the largest Aquarium in the world! And it is right there in Centennial Park. Spend some time learning about the sea life and water creatures alike.

All of this and more are just a stones throw from Centennial Park. Like I mentioned before, there are also seasonal events happening throughout the year. So be sure to save a day, or maybe two, to get in on all the action!

48. SWEET AUBURN

This neighborhood hosts a load of history and charm. Wander this little corner and you will be walking with the past. No matter if you are nostalgic for yester year, or like to get into the nitty gritty of the city, Sweet Auburn is a wonderful place to be.

The Sweet Auburn Curb Market established in 1923 is one of the most famous attractions in this neighborhood. Various merchants, vendors, and retailers fill the space to give customers and visitors a dazzling southern experience. The Curb Market is has a total of 24 individual businesses inside. My favorite is the Sweet Auburn Bakery.

49. WEST EGG

This hot spot is what breakfast dreams are made of, and it is here in Atlanta. Be sure to make a reservation because this place fills up quick. Prepare to have the best brunch of your life at West Egg.

My favorite thing to eat here is the Peachtree Plate. A bit of a chiché but worth the pun of ordering! This awesome dish has two of my favorites, brown sugar bacon and fried green tomato's, among other sides! Pair this with a classic mimosa and your about to go to brunch heaven! Check out West Egg on Instagram if you want to start feasting with the eyes before breakfast!

>TOURIST

50. PAINTED PIN

Cap off your trip with one last night on the town. Painted Pin is way more than a bowling ally. This place contains all the fun to entertain you and all your friends. Games, fun, and drinks are all top notch at the Painted Pin. It is sure to be a night you won't forget.

If you are not much of a bowler, like me, fear not! This fun house has something for you too. Make your way to the bar and get some refreshments before finding a game for you. Choose between giant jenga, darts, pool, or any other amenity they offer. You are sure to have fun with your friends hopping around the Painted Pin playing like kids again.

EVANS

>TOURIST

TOP REASONS TO BOOK THIS TRIP

People: Southern hospitality is real. You will feel like a local after the first "Hello sweetie!"

Food: The food scene in Atlanta is next level! Foodies welcome!

Urban meets rural: Get the best of both worlds in this perfectly located city.

EVANS

> TOURIST
GREATER THAN A TOURIST

Visit GreaterThanATourist.com:
http://GreaterThanATourist.com

Sign up for the Greater Than a Tourist Newsletter:
http://eepurl.com/cxspyf

Follow us on Facebook:
https://www.facebook.com/GreaterThanATourist

Follow us on Pinterest:
http://pinterest.com/GreaterThanATourist

Follow us on Instagram:
http://Instagram.com/GreaterThanATourist

EVANS

> TOURIST
GREATER THAN A TOURIST

Please leave your honest review of this book on Amazon and Goodreads. Thank you.

We appreciate your positive and negative feedback as we try to provide tourist guidance in their next trip from a local.

EVANS

>TOURIST

NOTES

Made in the USA
Columbia, SC
01 August 2021